Water

Sydnie Sawicki

BookLeaf Publishing

India | USA | UK

Presentation by *BookLeaf Publishing*

Web: www.bookleafpub.com

E-mail: info@bookleafpub.com

ISBN: 9789360945954

First edition 2024

This book is dedicated to my mom.

Even with all the words in the world, my love for you can never be truly expressed.

You have always been my biggest fan,

and have always loved my deep feelings and big emotions.

I love you. <3

This book is also dedicated to my grandmaw.

You are Love Embodied.

I love you more than words can say,

and that's all I know. :)

ACKNOWLEDGEMENT

A special thank you for all those involved with the publishing of this book.

And a special thank you to all the readers of this book.

Thank you.

Blossom

I don't want to fall in love.
Things that fall get broken.
I want to grow in love
Like flowers in a garden.
I'll water you
You water me,
And we'll watch each other blossom.

four a.m.

It's four a.m.
and I find myself awake, again.
Everything I never wanted to think
comes pouring in.
Like the relentless rain
against my windowpane.
Each drop
a thought
Rushing in like the floodgates collapsed,
no longer holding these emotions back.
I'm my most vulnerable
alone at four a.m.
When the world is still.

Little Things

It's the little things that make me think of you
I often wonder if you think of me, too.
I sometimes get lost
in the 'could have beens'
and the 'would have beens'
and it would be nice to see you again.
Would my heart skip a beat?
Would I want us to meet
for a chance to speak
just one more time?
Would we pick up like old times?
Y'know, with all of the smiles
and all of the jokes
and all of the laughter
Like, life didn't happen after all.

Sweet Girl

Oh, sweet girl
Why are you so sweet, girl?
Why are you so flawless
lost in thoughts
that make your lip curl?
A dreaming in the day girl.
Romanticizing fantasies
of a different world girl.
Your heart is gonna break, girl
This world is not that place, girl.
See, people treat each other
like another form of waste, girl.
Just taking what they can, girl.
Especially a man, girl.
Though, anyone will use you
and abuse your open hand, girl.

Summer Rain

5

I found myself standing at the kitchen sink,
staring out the window.
Trying to find any kind
of silver lining,
but all I found were thunderclouds.
Pouring rain.
The kind of rain
that looked like it could
wash his sins away.
His scent away.
You'd think with how loud the thunder was
it would drown out his voice.
His voice like thunder,
cracking away at my innocence.
His skin like scales
against my own.
I stood in silence
repeating the moment,
like the sound of thunder
in a summer storm.

I listened to the rain
ping against the tin roof,
until I finally made my way outside.
I let the rain wash over me,

Slowly cleansing me
from the outside in,
until I could no longer feel
his heat lingering against my skin.
Once more, I let the rain pour,
until one could no longer tell
rain drops from tear drops
or the crack of thunder from my breaking heart.

Tears

Liquid Emotion
carries words my heart can't say,
streaming down my face.

Water

Empty words and broken promises
was the glue that held us together
for so long.
If love is water
He was a drought,
never enough rain
to water my soul
and allow me to bloom.

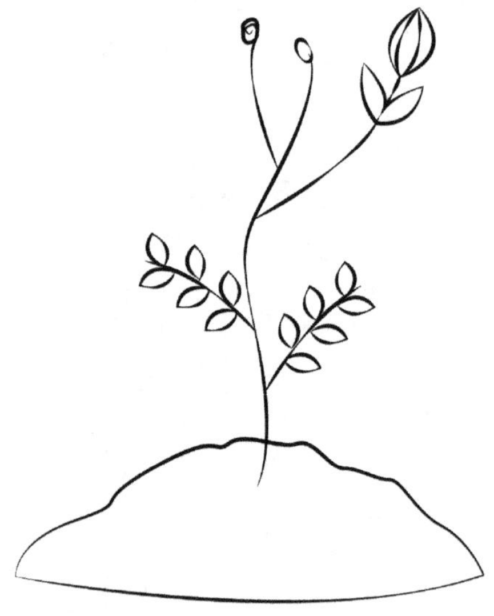

Beats

I used to think
being single
and wanting someone
made me desperate
for love. But imagine
going back
to that same toxic person
always hoping
for love. Y'know,
the ones that never
see their wrong. Always
playing the victim
like the beat
of a drum. I can count it
like beats
the same scene

that repeats.
One, two, three, four.
One, two, three, four.
Counting out to nothing more.
Always starting back at one
again. Always hoping
for a different end. It was good
in the beginning
because the hope
was there. The idea
of "what could be"
you cling onto, like air. Then
familiarness sets in
and you feel comfortable, again.
Getting back
into the swings of things, just
to get back
into the swing of things. Sounding
like beats
the same scene
that repeats. And again
you find yourself at 'four'
counting out
to nothing more.

I see you with
compassion, those
hoping for love but
can't break the pattern, those desperate

for love but can't
see the damage. The emotional scars
that's left behind. To all of the trauma,
you've made yourself blind.
Feeling comfort in consistency, and
knowing what the beat will bring, it's only
a matter of time before
you think, "That's exactly how
Love is supposed to be."
You've gotten used
to the beat of their drum. Thinking
If you start over,
your whole life
will come undone. But,
you've gone deaf to your own song.
Your beat is so unique!
You haven't heard it in how long?!
Oh, it's my favorite song!
The way your melody
makes me move, I wish
you could hear it
the way I do.
I wish you could see you
the way I do.
I see you without
all of the trauma
you hold. I see you beyond
all of the lies
you've been told.

Those lies are notes
that sound all wrong,
causing chaos
to the harmony
of your song. When you're not in-tune with
yourself
even the right notes sound wrong.
You have to find your key
Understand that
Life is a Grand Piano,
You create your own harmony.
Learn to love your melody
that's something different,
don't you see? Where
they are a drum
they only play one beat.
Oh, but the harmony
you bring! All of the notes
you can play, and all of the
chords you create!
Don't limit yourself to just
one beat,
when there're so many things
you can be! Explore
your Light and your Shadow keys,
There's a reason
for all of these notes
You see, the low
and the high, they intertwine

to make a beautiful melody.
Something so uniquely you,
nobody else
can sound like you! So,
step into your solo
and let your spotlight shine down, and
unapologetically play
your beautiful sound.

Imagination at Play

He came to see me today.
I guess He had some things to say.
So, I jotted them down, with great detail
Because the next time I see him -
Time will tell.
This relationship is love/hate.
Every time he leaves
I just have to wait.
Coming and going
whenever he please;
the emotional type,
He wears his heart on his sleeve.
He often gets around.
In every thing
he can be found. Everywhere
he goes, he leaves a spark. After all,
You can't spell Earth without Art.

He's creativity,
He's Creative Energy.
Bouncing around from place to place
keeping imagination at play.
But as quick as he comes
he leaves again,
off to see another friend.
While I sit patiently
for his next visit, like
"These words that I write, am I doing it right?"

Running Well

I have so many things
I want to say,
but sometimes
I don't know how to say it.
By the time
I get pen to paper
it's as if
all of these words
have faded. What was
once
a running well of words
has since
all about degraded,

and these trickle of lines
that I write
time to time
only leaves me
more frustrated. There's this
Energy inside
that's just
dying to be created,
when it's finally complete
I'm like,
"That was long awaited."
I try not to rush the process
or these words
will be sedated. Why have all these words
on paper, if my soul
won't be translated?
Getting back to poetry
is teaching me
the patience
I abated. A month at a time
to write some of these rhymes,
my spirits
would be deflated. But,
I've learned
that's it's the journey
where you need to be elated,
or you'll be arguing
the rules of a game
that you never

get to play it,
and eventually
the players will leave
and you'll be isolated. So,
I use these words
to process
the hurt
that I have integrated, and
each lesson learned is a page
that I have cultivated, until the day comes
and that poem is done,
and my Spirit is left exhilarated.

Only Human

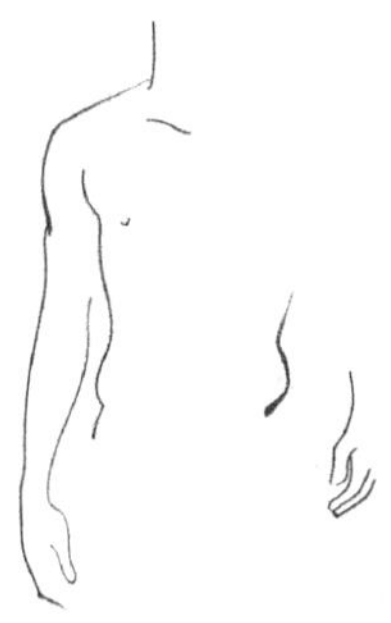

Why are you so hard on yourself?
So harsh,
So demanding,
So dismantling of yourself.
You criticize yourself,
overanalyze yourself.
Played victim too long
and antagonized yourself.
Your enemy
is the Negative Energy inside yourself.
You've got to accept yourself
and learn to respect yourself:
Embrace all of your space
and stop deflecting yourself.
'Cuz you'll always have to live with yourself,
So love and forgive yourself,
If not you could ruin yourself. After all,
You're only human, yourself.

Waiting

She sits with such patience.
Not moving a muscle
but ready to move at a moment's notice.
A little twitch of her tail,
She continues to watch.
with such diligence
patience
and readiness.
Not a rush in the world.
Just waiting
for the right moment
to pounce.

I wish I had
the patience of a cat.
No frustration
or irritation

with waiting.
No anxiety
from feeling like you're falling behind.
Just waiting
and watching,
with enough interest
and motive
and patience
to sit
with contentment.

Focus

I tried to stay focused today.
Instead, I thought about you
all day.
The way the sun glistens
off your dark brown skin.
The amber in your eyes
when the sun hits just right.
The gentleness in your voice
when we speak,
and the softness in your touch
when our skins meet.
The calmness you bring when you're around.
You're like nothing I've ever known
but have known for many lifetimes, now.

I hope I can mirror your softness.
Be a safe place
a safe space
for you to take off your armor.

ego

and when it's your Ego that gets in the way,
what do you do?
If it's not Ego,
it's fear, or criticism,
or fear of criticism.
Negative comments, or
people projecting their fears onto you.
So, what do you do?

Fight fear with wonder,
excitement,
and have the bravery of a child.
Be fearless,
and stay wild.

Calm in the Chaos

I find it so peaceful when it rains.
There's something so calming in the chaos.
The clashing of thunder
and flashing of lightning
brings comfort to my soul.
It's like Mother Nature
understands
all of these emotions
I sometimes can't control.
I've yelled like thunder
with words like lightning
lighting arguments ablaze
with my rage.
I've cried like rain.
Not a single sound to be heard
but the drops of pain.

Tears are words the heart can't say.
But it takes a little rain
for the flowers to grow,
and it takes a little pain
for the healing to show.
So, I go through phases, like the Moon.
I'm not always full of light,
sometimes, I have dark days, too.
Sometimes these days
turn into seasons
and the cold
frosts over my heart,
like Winter.
There are no flowers here.
Nothing ever blooms in the Winter
and I never
look forward
to Winter.
I'm more like Spring.
When Nature awakens from her cold slumber
and the coldness in my heart
thaws over. When the flowers bloom
I bloom, too.
Like the Dandelion,
I tend to chase the Wind
Following wherever it goes
and back again,
Sending my wishes
as whispers

to the Universe,
Praying one day
She sends them back.

Yet I often wonder how they feel
about the Winter
about the rain
about the darkness from which they came,
does it bring them pain, or
do they find comfort
in the escape?
Do they understand
the Storms are necessary
for change, or
is it just me
that struggles to see?

Solitude

I've found a comfort in my solitude,
and a blessing in the boredom.
Taking time to truly discover myself,
Solitude has given me
an opportunity.
To see myself.
To recreate myself.
No longer bound
by somebody's version of me.
I finally feel like I can breathe.

Yellow Trumpets

I felt the sun against my skin
with such a warmth, it was like
hugging an old friend.
The first warm day since last year.
Spring is near.
The daffodils like yellow trumpets
announcing Spring's return.
The Juneberry and Dogwood trees in full bloom.
The birds
singing Spring's song.

Spring brings renewal.
Hope
That there's life after perceived death.
Spring brings second chances.

Colors

You painted me red
and then said
I've shown my true colors. Like,
You never watched me cry blue so deep
the deep sea shutters.
Or the way I would shine so bright with yellow
when I'd smile.
You never saw the purple in me
when I would be inspired, or
the beaming ball of orange
burning with creativity.
You never felt
my grounding green Energy.

You never noticed my rainbow.
You only painted me red.

Passionfruit

They like comparing
apples to oranges, but I
am a passionfruit.

Balance

Calming and cleansing,
Destructive enough to drown.
Love is like Water.

Pages Untold

Do not look for me
in the pages of your memory,
I am no longer there.
Gone is the girl
too afraid to speak her truth,
Biting her tongue
so hard it would bleed.
Gone is the timid girl
whose back was more cartilage than bone.
Gone is the girl
afraid of being alone.

Do not look for me
in the pages of your memory.
Find me in the chapters untold,
Where worlds have yet to be written

into existence,
Where fantasies unfold.
Find me where stardust
and fairy dust collide -
where magick resides.

9 789360 945954